The Best Mediterranean Dinner Cookbook

Recipes For Easy And Tasty Mediterranean Dinners

Sommario

Introduction

In this book I want to give you all the most useful information to prepare fabulous dinners just in Mediterranean style.

Hard to forget dinners that you can share with friends, family or the person you love the most.

What could be better than a candlelight dinner to make the person you love fall in love with you?

And what better way than with typical Mediterranean dishes!

But let's not waste time and start learning and cooking... let's run to the kitchen and start.

Great Mediterranean Diet Recipes

Italian Herb Bread

Servings: 25

Cooking Time: 40 Minutes

Ingredients:

- 1 2/3 teaspoons active dry yeast

- 3½ cups all-purpose flour

- 2 1/4 cup rye flour

- 1 tablespoon salt

- 2 tablespoons olive oil

- 1 tablespoon flat-leaf parsley, finely chopped

- 10 sprigs fresh thyme leaves, stems removed

- 1 garlic clove, peeled and finely chopped

- ¼ cup black olives, pitted and chopped

- 3 green chilies, deseeded and chopped

- ¾ cup sun-dried tomatoes, drained and chopped

Directions:

1. Take a bowl of lukewarm water (temperature of 0 degrees F) and dissolve 1 and 2/3 cups of yeast.

2. Add flour, yeast water, and salt to another bowl.

3. Mix well to prepare the dough using a mixer or your hands.

4. Put the dough in a large, clean bowl and allow it to rest covered for 2 hours.

5. Transfer dough to a lightly floured surface and knead, adding the parsley, garlic, olives, thyme, tomatoes, and chilies.

6. Place the kneaded dough in an 8½-inch bread-proofing basket.

7. Cover and allow to rest for about 60 minutes.

8. Preheat oven to 400 degrees F.

9. Line a baking sheet with parchment paper.

10. Bake for about 30-40 minutes.

11. Once done, enjoy it!

Nutrition Info:Per Serving: Calories: 338, Total Fat: 2.5 g, Saturated Fat: 0.4 g, Cholesterol: 0 mg, Sodium: 294 mg, Total Carbohydrate: 68.6 g, Dietary Fiber: 5.5 g, Total Sugars: 0.5 g, Protein: 10 g, Vitamin D: 0 mcg, Calcium: 53 mg, Iron: 7 mg, Potassium: 202 mg

Kidney Bean, Veggie, And Grape Salad With Feta

Servings:4

Cooking Time: 25 Minutes

Ingredients:

- 1½ cups red grapes, halved

- 1 (15-ounce) can red kidney beans, drained and rinsed

- 10 ounces cherry tomatoes, halved (quartered if tomatoes are large)

- 4 (6-inch) Persian cucumbers, quartered vertically and chopped

- ½ cup green pumpkin seeds (pepitas)

- ½ cup feta cheese

- 2½ ounces baby spinach leaves (about 4 cups)

- ½ cup Dijon Red Wine Vinaigrette

Directions:

1. Place the grapes, kidney beans, cherry tomatoes, cucumbers, pumpkin seeds, and feta in a large mixing bowl and mix to combine.

2. Place cups of the salad mixture in each of 4 containers. Then place 1 cup of spinach leaves on top of each salad. Pour 2 tablespoons of

vinaigrette into each of 4 sauce containers. Refrigerate all the containers.

3. STORAGE: Store covered containers in the refrigerator for up to 5 days.

Nutrition Info:Per Serving: Total calories: 5; Total fat: 25g; Saturated fat: 6g; Sodium: 435mg; Carbohydrates: 37g; Fiber: 10g; Protein: 16g

Sumac Chickpea Bowl

Servings: 4

Cooking Time: 25 Minutes

Ingredients:

- ⅔ cup uncooked bulgur

- 1⅓ cups water

- ⅛ teaspoon kosher salt

- 1 teaspoon olive oil

- 2 tablespoons olive oil

- 2 (15.5-ounce) cans low-sodium chickpeas, drained and rinsed

- 3 tablespoons sumac

- ¼ teaspoon kosher salt

- 4 Persian cucumbers, quartered lengthwise and chopped (about 2 cups)

- 10 ounces cherry tomatoes, quartered (halved if you have small tomatoes)

- ¼ cup chopped fresh mint

- 1 cup chopped fresh parsley

- 4 teaspoons olive oil

- 2 tablespoons plus 2 teaspoons freshly squeezed lemon juice

- ¼ teaspoon kosher salt

- 2 tablespoons unsalted tahini

- ¼ teaspoon garlic powder

- 5 tablespoons water

Directions:

1. TO MAKE THE BULGUR

2. Place the bulgur, water, and salt in a saucepan, and bring to a boil. Once it boils, cover the pot with a lid and turn off the heat. Let the covered pot stand for minutes. Stir the oil into the cooked bulgur. Cool.

3. Place ½ cup of bulgur in each of 4 microwaveable containers.

4. TO MAKE THE CHICKPEAS

5. Heat the oil in a 12-inch skillet over medium-high heat. Once the oil is shimmering, add the chickpeas, sumac, and salt, and stir to coat. Cook for 2 minutes without stirring. Give the

chickpeas a stir and cook for another 2 minutes without stirring. Stir and cook for 2 more minutes.

6. Place ¾ cup of cooled chickpeas in each of the 4 bulgur containers.

7. TO MAKE THE SALAD

8. Combine all the ingredients for the salad in a medium mixing bowl. Taste for salt and lemon, and add more if you need it.

9. Place 1¼ cup of salad in each of 4 containers. These containers will not be reheated.

10. TO MAKE THE TAHINI SAUCE

11. Combine the tahini and garlic powder in a small bowl. Whisk in 1 tablespoon of water at a time until all 5 tablespoons have been incorporated and a thin sauce has formed. It will thicken as it sits.

12.   Place 1 tablespoon of tahini sauce in each of 4 small sauce containers.

13.   STORAGE: Store covered containers in the refrigerator for up to 5 days. When serving, reheat the bulgur and chickpeas, add them to the salad, and drizzle the tahini sauce over the top.

Nutrition Info:Per Serving: Total calories: 485; Total fat: 19g; Saturated fat: 2g; Sodium: 361mg; Carbohydrates: 67g; Fiber: 19g; Protein: 16g

Smoked Salmon And Lemon-dill Ricotta Bento Box

Servings: 4

Cooking Time: 10 Minutes

Ingredients:

- FOR THE LEMON-DILL RICOTTA

- 1 (16-ounce) container whole-milk ricotta cheese

- 1 teaspoon finely grated lemon zest

- 3 tablespoons chopped fresh dill

- FOR THE BENTO BOX

- 8 ounces smoked salmon

- 4 (6-inch) Persian cucumbers or 2 small European cucumbers, sliced

- 2 cups sugar snap peas

- 4 whole-wheat pitas, each cut into 4 pieces

Directions:

1. Mix all the ingredients for the lemon-dill ricotta in a medium bowl.

2. Divide the salmon, cucumbers, and snap peas among 4 containers.

3. Place 1 pita in each of 4 resealable bags.

4. Place ½ cup of ricotta spread in each of separate small containers, since it may release some liquid after a couple of days.

5. STORAGE: Store covered containers in the refrigerator for up to 4 days. Store the pita at room temperature or in the refrigerator.

Nutrition Info:Per Serving: Total calories: 4; Total fat: 20g; Saturated fat: 11g; Sodium: 1,388mg; Carbohydrates: 40g; Fiber: 8g; Protein: 32g

Mediterranean Baked Tilapia With Roasted Baby Red Potatoes

Servings: 2

Cooking Time: 35 Minutes

Ingredients:

- 3 teaspoons olive oil, divided

- 1 small yellow onion, very thinly sliced (about 2½ cups)

- 1 large red bell pepper, thinly sliced (about 2 cups)

- 10 ounces baby red potatoes, quartered (about 1-inch pieces)

- ⅜ teaspoon kosher salt, divided

- 1 teaspoon chopped garlic

- 1 tablespoon capers, drained, rinsed, and roughly chopped

- ¼ cup golden raisins

- 1 (½-ounce) pack fresh basil, roughly chopped

- 2½ ounces baby spinach, large leaves torn in half (about 4 cups)

- 2 teaspoons freshly squeezed lemon juice

- 8 ounces tilapia or other thin white fish (see tip)

Directions:

1. Preheat the oven to 450°F. Line a sheet pan with a silicone baking mat or parchment paper.

2. Heat teaspoons of oil in a 12-inch skillet over medium heat. When the oil is shimmering, add the onions and peppers. Cook for 12 minutes, stirring occasionally. The onions should be very soft.

3. While the onions and peppers are cooking, place the potatoes on the sheet pan and toss with ⅛ teaspoon of salt and the remaining 1 teaspoon of oil. Spread the potatoes out evenly across half of the pan. Roast in the oven for 10 minutes.

4. Once the onions are soft, add the garlic, capers, raisins, basil, ⅛ teaspoon of salt, and the spinach. Stir to combine and cook for 3 more minutes to wilt the spinach.

5. Carefully remove the sheet pan from the oven after 10 minutes. Add half of the onion mixture to the empty side of the pan to form a nest for the fish. Place the fish on top and season with the remaining ⅛ teaspoon of salt and the lemon juice. Spread the rest of the onion mixture evenly across the top of the fish.

6. Place the pan back in the oven and cook for 10 minutes. The fish should be flaky.

7. When the fish and potatoes have cooled, place 1 piece of fish plus half of the potatoes and half of the onion mixture in each of 2 containers. Refrigerate.

8. STORAGE: Store covered containers in the refrigerator for up to 4 days.

Nutrition Info:Per Serving: Total calories: 427; Total fat: ; Saturated fat: 2g; Sodium: 952mg; Carbohydrates: 59g; Fiber: 10g; Protein: 31g

Mediterranean Focaccia

Servings: 4

Cooking Time: 30 Minutes

Ingredients:

- 3 3/5 cups flour

- 1 1/7 cups warm water

- 2 tablespoons olive oil

- 2 teaspoons dry yeast

- 1½ teaspoons salt

- 1 cup black olives, pitted and coarsely chopped

- sea salt

- olive oil

Directions:

1. Place flour and yeast in a large bowl.

2. Make a well and pour in water, salt, and oil.

3. Gradually keep mixing until everything is incorporated well.

4. Knead for about 20 minutes.

5. Add black olives and mix well.

6. Form a ball and allow it to rise for about 45 minutes (in a bowl covered with a towel).

7. Once the dough is ready, push air out of it by crushing it using your palm.

8. Roll out the dough onto a floured surface to a thickness of about ½ an inch.

9. Place it on a baking sheet covered with parchment paper, and allow the dough to rise for another 45 minutes.

10.   Preheat oven to 425 degrees Fahrenheit.

11. Press fingers into the dough at regular intervals to pierce the dough.

12. When ready to bake, pour a bit of olive oil into the holes and sprinkle with salt.

13. Bake for 20-30 minutes.

14. Enjoy!

Nutrition Info:Per Serving: Calories: 523, Total Fat: 11.7 g, Saturated Fat: 1.7 g, Cholesterol: 0 mg, Sodium: 3495 mg, Total Carbohydrate: 89.4 g, Dietary Fiber: 4.6 g, Total Sugars: 0.3 g, Protein: 13.8 g, Vitamin D: 0 mcg, Calcium: 50 mg, Iron: 7 mg, Potassium: 124 mg

Cheesy Olive Bread

Servings: 8

Cooking Time: 15 Minutes

Ingredients:

- ½ cup softened butter

- ¼ cup mayo

- 1 teaspoon garlic powder

- 1 teaspoon onion powder

- 2 cups shredded mozzarella cheese

- ½ cup chopped black olives

- 1 loaf of French Bread, halved longways

Directions:

1. Preheat oven to a temperature of 350 degrees Fahrenheit.

2. Stir butter and mayo together in a bowl until it is smooth and creamy.

3. Add onion powder, garlic powder, olives, and cheese and stir.

4. Spread the mixture over French bread.

5. Place bread on a baking sheet and bake for 10-12 minutes.

6. Increase the heat to broil and cook until the cheese has melted and the bread is golden brown.

7. Cool and chill.

8. Pre-heat before eating.

Nutrition Info:Per Serving: Calories: 307, Total Fat: 17.7 g, Saturated Fat: 2 g, Cholesterol: 38 mg, Sodium: 482 mg, Total Carbohydrate: 30.1 g, Dietary Fiber: 1.5 g, Total Sugars: 1.9 g, Protein: 8 g, Vitamin D: 0 mcg, Calcium: 40 mg, Iron: 2 mg, Potassium: 73 mg

Red Wine–marinated Flank Steak With Brussels Sprout Slaw

Servings: 2

Cooking Time: 10 Minutes

Ingredients:

- FOR THE STEAK

- 8 ounces flank steak, trimmed of visible fat

- ½ cup red wine

- 2 tablespoons low-sodium soy sauce

- 1 tablespoon olive oil

- ½ teaspoon garlic powder

- FOR THE BRUSSELS SPROUT SLAW

- 8 ounces Brussels sprouts, stemmed, halved, and very thinly sliced

- 3 tablespoons unsalted sunflower seeds

- 3 tablespoons freshly squeezed lemon juice

- 1 tablespoon plus 1 teaspoon olive oil

- 2 tablespoons dried cranberries

- ⅛ teaspoon kosher salt

- ⅔ cup Artichoke-Olive Compote

Directions:

1. TO MAKE THE STEAK

2. Place all the ingredients for the steak in a gallon-size resealable bag. Allow the steak to marinate overnight or up to hours.

3. Place the oven rack about 6 inches from the heating element. Preheat the oven to the broil setting (use the high setting if you have multiple settings).

4. Cover a sheet pan with foil. Lift the steak out of the marinade and place on top of the foil-lined sheet pan. Place the pan in the oven and cook for to 6 minutes on one side. Flip the steak over to the other side and broil for 4 to 6 minutes more.

5. Remove from the oven and allow to rest for to 10 minutes. Medium-rare will be about 135°F when an instant-read meat thermometer is inserted.

6. On a cutting board, slice the steak thinly against the grain and divide the steak between 2 containers.

7. TO MAKE THE BRUSSELS SPROUT SLAW

8. Combine the Brussels sprouts, sunflower seeds, lemon juice, olive oil, cranberries, and salt in a medium bowl.

9. Place 1 cup of Brussels sprout slaw and ⅓ cup of artichoke-olive compote in each of 2 containers. The slaw and compote are meant to

be eaten at room temperature, while the steak can be eaten warm. However, if you want to eat the steak at room temperature as well, all the items can be put in the same container.

10. STORAGE: Store covered containers in the refrigerator for up to 5 days.

Nutrition Info:Per Serving: Total calories: 601; Total fat: 31g; Saturated fat: 3g; Sodium: 1,098mg; Carbohydrates: 26g; Fiber: 5g; Protein: 29g

One-pot Spanish Chicken Sausage And Shrimp With Rice

Servings: 4

Cooking Time: 30 Minutes

Ingredients:

- 4 teaspoons olive oil, divided

- 1 (12-ounce) package cooked chicken sausage, sliced

- 6 ounces uncooked peeled, deveined medium shrimp

- 1 large green bell pepper, chopped (about 1½ cups)

- 1 small yellow onion, chopped (about 2 cups)

- 2 teaspoons chopped garlic

- 2 teaspoons smoked paprika

- 1 teaspoon dried thyme leaves

- 1 teaspoon dried oregano

- ½ teaspoon kosher salt

- ½ cup quick-cooking or instant brown rice

- 1 (14.5-ounce) can no-salt-added diced tomatoes in juice

- 1 cup low-sodium chicken broth

- 1 medium zucchini, halved vertically and sliced into half-moons

Directions:

1. Heat 2 teaspoons of oil in a soup pot over medium-high heat. When the oil is shimmering, add the sausage and brown for 5 minutes. Add the shrimp and cook for more minute. Remove the sausage and shrimp, and place them on a plate.

2. Add the remaining teaspoons of oil to the pot, and when the oil is shimmering, add the bell pepper, onion, and garlic. Sauté until soft, about 5 minutes.

3. Add the sausage, shrimp, paprika, thyme, oregano, salt, rice, tomatoes, and broth to the pot, and stir to combine. Bring to a boil, then cover the pot and turn the heat down to low. Simmer for 15 minutes.

4. After 15 minutes, add the zucchini, return the cover to the pot, and continue to simmer for 5 to 10 more minutes, until the zucchini is crisp-tender and the rice has absorbed most of the liquid.

5. Place about 2 cups of the rice mixture in each of 4 containers.

6. STORAGE: Store covered containers in the refrigerator for up to 5 days.

Nutrition Info:Per Serving: Total calories: 333; Total fat: 14g; Saturated fat: 3g; Sodium: 954mg; Carbohydrates: 29g; Fiber: 6g; Protein: 26g

Broccoli, Roasted Red Pepper, Cheddar, And Olive Frittata

Servings: 5

Cooking Time: 25 Minutes

Ingredients:

- Oil or cooking spray for greasing the pan

- 8 large eggs

- ½ cup low-fat (2%) milk

- 1 teaspoon smoked paprika

- 6 ounces broccoli florets, finely chopped (about 2 cups)

- ½ cup chopped jarred roasted red peppers, drained of liquid

- ⅓ cup pitted black olives, chopped (or other olive of your choice)

- ¼ cup shredded sharp Cheddar cheese, plus 2 tablespoons

Directions:

1. Preheat the oven to 375°F and rub an 8-inch round cake or pie pan with oil, or spray with cooking spray.

2. Break the eggs into a large mixing bowl. Add the milk and smoked paprika, and whisk until well combined.

3. Add the chopped broccoli, red peppers, olives, and ¼ cup of cheese, and mix.

4. Pour the mixture into the oiled pan and top with the remaining 2 tablespoons of cheese. Bake for 20 to 25 minutes.

5. Once the frittata is cool, run a spatula around the sides and slice into pieces.

6. Place 1 slice in each of 5 containers and refrigerate.

7. STORAGE: Store covered containers in the refrigerator for up to 5 days.

Nutrition Info:Per Serving: Total calories: 193; Total fat: 12g; Saturated fat: 5g; Sodium: 295mg; Carbohydrates: 7g; Fiber: 1g; Protein: 13g

Chutney-dijon Pork Tenderloin With Mushroom And Kale Farro Pilaf

Servings: 2

Cooking Time: 40 Minutes

Ingredients:

- 8 ounces pork tenderloin (freeze half if you can only find a 1-pound package)

- ⅓ cup prepared mango or apricot chutney, plus 1 tablespoon

- 2 tablespoons Dijon mustard

- 1 teaspoon chopped garlic

- 2 teaspoons olive oil

- 2 teaspoons olive oil

- 4 ounces mushrooms, sliced

- 1 small bunch (about 7 ounces) lacinato or curly kale, ribs removed, leaves roughly chopped

- ½ teaspoon chopped garlic

- ⅔ cup farro

- ¼ cup dry red wine, such as red zinfandel, merlot, or cabernet

- 1¼ cups low-sodium vegetable broth (or chicken broth)

- ¼ teaspoon kosher salt

Directions:

1. TO MAKE THE PORK

2. Remove the tough silver skin from the tenderloin with a sharp knife.

3. In a small bowl, combine ⅓ cup of chutney and the mustard, garlic, and oil.

4. Place the pork in a gallon-size resealable bag or shallow dish and rub the chutney mixture over the pork. Marinate for at least 8 hours.

5. When you're ready to cook, preheat the oven to 0°F and line a sheet pan with a silicone baking mat or foil.

6. Remove the pork from the marinade and place it on the sheet pan. Discard the marinade. Place the pork in the oven for 10 minutes. Turn it over, rub the remaining 1 tablespoon of chutney over the top and sides, and roast for another 8 minutes. (Don't worry if extra marinade burns on the baking mat. The pork will be okay.)

7. Let the pork cool for at least 10 minutes and slice.

8. Divide the slices between 2 containers.

9. TO MAKE THE MUSHROOM AND KALE FARRO PILAF

10.   Heat the oil in a soup pot or Dutch oven over medium-high heat. When the oil is shimmering, add the mushrooms and cook for 4 minutes.

11.   Add the kale and garlic, stir, and cook for another 5 minutes.

12.   Add the farro, stir, and cook for 1 minute. Add the red wine and allow to cook for 1 more minute.

13.   Add the broth and salt, increase the heat to high, and bring to a boil. Once it is boiling, turn the heat down to low, cover, and simmer for 30 minutes, until the farro is tender but still has some bite to it.

14.   After it has cooled, place 1 heaping cup of pilaf in each of the 2 pork containers. Refrigerate.

15.   STORAGE: Store covered containers in the refrigerator for up to 5 days. Freeze farro pilaf for up to 6 months.

Nutrition Info:Per Serving: Total calories: 677; Total fat: 18g; Saturated fat: 3g; Sodium: 1,041mg; Carbohydrates: 76g; Fiber: 10g; Protein: 48g

Tuna, Kale Slaw, Edamame, And Strawberry Salad

Servings: 3

Cooking Time: 15 Minutes

Ingredients:

- 2 (5-ounce) cans light tuna packed in water

- 8 tablespoons Honey-Lemon Vinaigrette, divided

- 3 cups prepackaged kale-and-cabbage slaw

- 1 cup shelled frozen edamame, thawed

- 2 Persian cucumbers, quartered vertically and chopped

- 1¼ cups sliced strawberries

- 3 tablespoons chopped fresh dill

Directions:

1. Place the tuna in a small bowl and mix with 2 tablespoons of vinaigrette.

2. In a large mixing bowl, place the slaw, edamame, cucumbers, strawberries, and dill. Toss to combine.

3. Place ⅓ cup of tuna in each of containers. Place one third of the salad on top of the tuna in each container to lessen the chance of the salad getting soggy. Spoon 2 tablespoons of the remaining vinaigrette into each of 3 separate sauce containers.

4. STORAGE: Store covered containers in the refrigerator for up to days.

Nutrition Info:Per Serving: Total calories: 317; Total fat: 18g; Saturated fat: 2g; Sodium: 414mg; Carbohydrates: 22g; Fiber: 9g; Protein: 22g

Avocado Green Goddess Dip With Veggie Dippers

Servings: 4

Cooking Time: 10 Minutes

Ingredients:

- ½ teaspoon chopped garlic

- 1 cup packed fresh parsley leaves

- ½ cup fresh mint leaves

- ¼ cup fresh tarragon leaves

- ¼ teaspoon plus ⅛ teaspoon kosher salt

- ¼ cup freshly squeezed lemon juice

- ¼ cup extra-virgin olive oil

- ½ cup water

- 1 medium avocado

- 1 (1-pound) bag baby carrots

- 2 heads endive, leaves separated

Directions:

1. Place the garlic, parsley, mint, tarragon, salt, lemon juice, oil, water, and avocado in a blender and blend until smooth.

2. Place 4 ounces of carrots and half a head of endive leaves in each of 4 containers. Spoon ¼ cup of dip into each of 4 sauce containers.

3. STORAGE: Store covered containers in the refrigerator for up to 5 days.

Nutrition Info:Per Serving: Total calories: 301; Total fat: 21g; Saturated fat: 2g; Sodium: 373mg; Carbohydrates: 2; Fiber: 13g; Protein: 23g

Black Olive Bread

Servings: 6

Cooking Time: 45 Minutes

Ingredients:

- 3 cups bread flour

- 2 teaspoons active dry yeast

- 2 tablespoons white sugar

- 1 teaspoon salt

- ½ cup black olives, chopped

- 3 tablespoons olive oil

- 1¼ cups warm water (about 110 degrees Fahrenheit)

- 1 tablespoon cornmeal

Directions:

1. In a large bowl, combine flour, sugar, yeast, salt, black olives, water, and olive oil.

2. Mix well to prepare the dough.

3. Turn the dough onto a floured surface and knead well for 5-10 minutes until elastic.

4. Set dough aside and allow it to rise for about minutes until it has doubled in size.

5. Punch the dough down and knead again for 10 minutes.

6. Allow it to rise for 30 minutes more.

7. Round up the dough on a kneading board, place upside down in a bowl, and line it with a lint-free, well-floured towel.

8. Allow it to rise until it has doubled in size again.

9. While the bread is rising up for the third and final time, take a pan, fill it up with water, and place it at the bottom of your oven.

10. Preheat oven to a temperature of 500 degrees Fahrenheit.

11. Turn the loaf out onto a sheet pan, lightly oil it, and dust with cornmeal.

12. Bake for about 15 minutes.

13. Reduce heat to 375 degrees Fahrenheit and bake for another 30 minutes.

14. Cool and chill.

15. Enjoy!

Nutrition Info:Per Serving: Calories: 324, Total Fat: 8.9 g, Saturated Fat: 1.3 g, Cholesterol: 0 mg, Sodium: 488 mg, Total Carbohydrate: 53.9 g, Dietary Fiber: 2.4 g, Total Sugars: 4.2 g, Protein: 7.2 g, Vitamin D: 0 mcg, Calcium: 20 mg, Iron: 4 mg, Potassium: 98 mg

Cocoa-almond Bliss Bites

Servings: 10

Cooking Time: 1 Hour

Ingredients:

- 1 medium ripe banana, mashed

- 3 tablespoons ground flaxseed

- ½ cup rolled oats

- ½ cup plain, unsalted almond butter

- 2 tablespoons unsweetened cocoa powder

- ¼ cup almond meal

- ¼ teaspoon ground cinnamon

- 2 teaspoons pure maple syrup

Directions:

1. Combine all the ingredients in a medium mixing bowl.

2. Roll the mixture into 10 balls, slightly smaller than a golf ball, and place on a plate.

3. Freeze the bites for 1 hour to harden.

4. Place 2 bites in each of 5 small containers or resealable bags and store in the refrigerator.

5. STORAGE: Store covered containers or resealable bags in the refrigerator for up to days. If you want to make a big batch, the bites can be frozen for up to 3 months.

6. Nutrition Info:Per Serving (2 bites): Total calories: 130; Total fat: 9g; Saturated fat: 1g; Sodium: 1mg; Carbohydrates: 11g; Fiber: 3g; Protein: 5g

Crispbread With Mascarpone And Berry-chia Jam

Servings: 3

Cooking Time: 5 Minutes

Ingredients:

- 1 (1-pound) bag frozen mixed berries

- 2 teaspoons freshly squeezed lemon juice

- 2 teaspoons pure maple syrup

- 2 tablespoons plus 2 teaspoons chia seeds

- 6 slices crispbread

- 3 tablespoons mascarpone cheese

Directions:

1. Place the frozen berries in a saucepan over medium heat. When the berries are defrosted,

about 5 minutes, mash with a potato masher. You can leave them chunky.

2. Turn the heat off and add the lemon juice, maple syrup, and chia seeds.

3. Allow the jam to cool, then place in the refrigerator to thicken for about an hour.

4. Place 2 slices of crispbread in each of 3 resealable sandwich bags. Place 1 tablespoon of mascarpone and 2 tablespoons of jam in each of 3 containers with dividers. Alternatively, put the mascarpone and jam in separate small sauce containers.

5. STORAGE: Store crispbread at room temperature and jam and mascarpone in the refrigerator. Mascarpone will last for 7 days in the refrigerator, while jam will last for 2 weeks. Jam can be frozen for up to 3 months.

Nutrition Info:Per Serving: Total calories: 2; Total fat: 9g; Saturated fat: 3g; Sodium: 105mg; Carbohydrates: 40g; Fiber: 14g; Protein: 6g

Spiced Chicken-stuffed Zucchini With Brown Rice And Lentils

Servings: 3

Cooking Time: 35 Minutes

Ingredients:

- ⅓ cup long-grain brown rice

- 1⅔ cups water

- ⅛ teaspoon kosher salt

- ⅓ cup brown lentils

- 2 teaspoons olive oil

- 3 tablespoons chopped fresh dill

- 3 medium zucchini, halved lengthwise and flesh scooped out with a teaspoon (zucchini flesh reserved)

- 3 teaspoons olive oil, divided

- 1 small yellow onion, chopped

- 1 teaspoon chopped garlic

- ½ pound ground lean chicken

- ¾ teaspoon ground cumin

- ¾ teaspoon ground coriander

- ¾ teaspoon caraway seeds

- ⅛ teaspoon red chili flakes

- 3 tablespoons tomato paste

- ¼ teaspoon kosher salt

- ¼ cup feta cheese

Directions:

1. TO MAKE THE BROWN RICE AND LENTILS

2. Place the rice, water, and salt in a saucepan over high heat. Once the water is boiling, cover

the pan and reduce the heat to low. Simmer for 15 minutes.

3. After 15 minutes, add the lentils and stir. Cover the pan and cook for another 15 minutes.

4. If there is a little bit of water still in the pan after the rice and lentils are tender, cook uncovered for a couple of minutes.

5. Stir in the oil and chopped dill.

6. Once the mixture has cooled, place ⅔ cup in each of 3 containers.

7. TO MAKE THE STUFFED ZUCCHINI

8. Preheat the oven to 400°F and line a sheet pan with a silicone baking mat or parchment paper. Place the zucchini boats on a lined sheet pan and coat with 1 teaspoon of oil.

9. In a 12-inch skillet, heat the remaining 2 teaspoons of oil over medium-high heat. When the oil is shimmering, add the onion and garlic

and cook for 5 minutes. Add the zucchini flesh and cook for 2 more minutes.

10. Add the ground chicken, breaking it up with a spatula. Cook for 5 more minutes.

11. Add the cumin, coriander, caraway seeds, chili flakes, tomato paste, and salt, and cook for another 2 minutes.

12. Mound the chicken mixture into the zucchini boats. Top each zucchini boat with 2 teaspoons of feta cheese. Bake for 20 minutes.

13. Once cooled, place 2 zucchini halves in each of the 3 rice-and-lentil containers.

14. STORAGE: Store covered containers in the refrigerator for up to 5 days. Brown rice and lentils can be frozen for up to 3 months.

Nutrition Info:Per Serving: Total calories: 414; Total fat: 19g; Saturated fat: 5g; Sodium: 645mg; Carbohydrates: 39g; Fiber: 10g; Protein: 26g

Apple, Cinnamon, And Walnut Baked Oatmeal

Servings: 8

Cooking Time: 40 Minutes

Ingredients:

- Cooking spray or oil for greasing the pan

- 3 small Granny Smith apples (about 1 pound), skin-on, chopped into ½-inch dice

- 3 cups rolled oats

- 1 teaspoon baking powder

- 3 tablespoons ground flaxseed

- 1 teaspoon ground cinnamon

- 2 eggs

- ¼ cup olive oil

- 1½ cups low-fat (2%) milk

- ⅓ cup pure maple syrup

- ½ cup walnut pieces (if you buy walnut halves, roughly chop the nuts)

Directions:

1. Preheat the oven to 350°F and spray an 8-by-inch baking dish with cooking spray or rub with oil.

2. Combine the apples, oats, baking powder, flaxseed, cinnamon, eggs, oil, milk, and maple

syrup in a large mixing bowl and pour into the prepared baking dish.

3. Sprinkle the walnut pieces evenly across the oatmeal and bake for 40 minutes.

4. Allow the oatmeal to cool and cut it into 8 pieces. Place 1 piece in each of 5 containers. Take the other 3 pieces and either eat as a snack during the week or freeze for a later time.

5. STORAGE: Store covered containers in the refrigerator for up to 6 days. If frozen, oatmeal will last 6 months.

Nutrition Info:Per Serving: Total calories: 349; Total fat: 18g; Saturated fat: 3g; Sodium: 108mg; Carbohydrates: 43g; Fiber: ; Protein: 9g

Chocolate–peanut Butter Yogurt With Berries

Servings: 4

Cooking Time: 15 Minutes

Ingredients:

- 2 cups low-fat (2%) plain Greek yogurt

- 4 tablespoons unsweetened cocoa powder

- 4 tablespoons natural-style peanut butter

- 1 tablespoon pure maple syrup

- 1 cup fresh or frozen berries of your choice

Directions:

1. In a medium bowl, mix the yogurt, cocoa powder, peanut butter, and maple syrup until well combined.

2. Spoon ½ cup of the yogurt mixture and ¼ cup of berries into each of 4 containers.

3. STORAGE: Store covered containers in the refrigerator for up to 5 days.

Nutrition Info:Per Serving: Total calories: 225; Total fat: 12g; Saturated fat: ; Sodium: 130mg; Carbohydrates: 19g; Fiber: 4g; Protein: 16g

Olive Fougasse

Servings: 4

Cooking Time: 20 Minutes

Ingredients:

- 3 2/3 cups bread flour

- 3 1/2 tablespoons olive oil

- 1 2/3 tablespoons bread yeast

- 1 1/4 cups black olives, chopped

- 1 teaspoon oregano

- 1 teaspoon salt

- 1 cup water

Directions:

1. Add flour to a bowl.

2. Make a well in the center and add the water and remaining Ingredients:.

3. Knead the dough well until it becomes slightly elastic.

4. Mold it into a ball and let stand for about 1 hour.

5. Divide the pastry into four pieces of equal portions.

6. Flatten the balls using a rolling pin and place it on a floured baking tray.

7. Make incisions on the bread.

8. Allow them to rest for about 30 minutes

9. Preheat oven to 425 degrees Fahrenheit.

10. Brush the Fougasse with olive oil and allow it to bake for 20 minutes.

11. Turn the oven off and allow it to rest for 5 minutes.

12. Remove and allow it to cool.

13. Enjoy!

Nutrition Info:Per Serving: Calories: 586, Total Fat: 18.1 g, Saturated Fat: 2.6 g, Cholesterol: 0 mg, Sodium: 371 mg, Total Carbohydrate: 92.2 g, Dietary Fiber: 5.6 g, Total Sugars: 0.3 g, Protein: 2 g, Vitamin D: 0 mcg, Calcium: 63 mg, Iron: 8 mg, Potassium: 232 mg

Tofu And Vegetable Provençal

Servings: 4

Cooking Time: 30 Minutes

Ingredients:

- 1 pound super-firm tofu, cut into ¾-inch cubes

- 2 tablespoons freshly squeezed lemon juice

- 2 tablespoons olive oil

- 1 teaspoon garlic powder

- 1 teaspoon herbes de Provence

- ¼ teaspoon kosher salt

- 4 teaspoons olive oil, divided

- 1 (14-ounce) eggplant, cubed into 1-inch pieces (5 to 6 cups)

- 1 small yellow onion, chopped (about 2 cups)

- 2 teaspoons chopped garlic

- 10 ounces cherry tomatoes, halved if tomatoes are fairly large

- 1 (14-ounce) can artichoke hearts, drained

- 1 teaspoon herbes de Provence

- ¼ teaspoon kosher salt

- ½ cup dry white wine, such as sauvignon blanc

- ⅓ cup pitted kalamata olives, roughly chopped

- 1 (½-ounce) package fresh basil, chopped

Directions:

1. TO MAKE THE TOFU

2. Place the tofu in a container with the lemon juice, oil, garlic powder, herbes de Provence, and salt. Allow to marinate for 1 hour.

3. When you're ready to cook the tofu, preheat the oven to 400°F and line a sheet pan with a silicone baking mat or parchment paper. Lift the tofu out of the marinade and place it on the sheet pan. Bake for minutes, flipping the tofu over after 15 minutes. Cool, then place about ½ cup of tofu cubes in each of 4 containers.

4. TO MAKE THE VEGETABLE RAGOUT

5. While the tofu is marinating, heat 2 teaspoons of oil in a 12-inch skillet over medium-high heat. When the oil is shimmering, add the eggplant and cook for 4 minutes, stirring

occasionally. Remove the eggplant and place on a plate.

6. Add the remaining 2 teaspoons of oil to the pan, and add the onion and garlic. Cook for 2 minutes. Add the tomatoes and cook for 5 more minutes. Add the eggplant, artichokes, herbes de Provence, salt, and wine. Cover the pan, lower the heat, and simmer for 20 minutes.

7. Turn the heat off and stir in the olives and basil.

8. Spoon about 1½ cups of vegetables into each of the 4 tofu containers.

9. STORAGE: Store covered containers in the refrigerator for up to 5 days.

Nutrition Info:Per Serving: Total calories: 362; Total fat: 17g; Saturated fat: 3g; Sodium: 728mg; Carbohydrates: 32g; Fiber: 9g; Protein: 23g

Banana, Orange, And Pistachio Smoothie

Servings: 3

Cooking Time: 25 Minutes

Ingredients:

- 1 (17.6-ounce) container plain low-fat (2%) Greek yogurt

- 3 very ripe medium bananas

- 1½ cups orange juice

- ¾ cup unsalted shelled pistachios

Directions:

1. Place all the ingredients in a blender and blend until smooth.

2. Pour 1¾ cups of the smoothie into each of 3 smoothie containers.

3. STORAGE: Store covered containers in the refrigerator for up to 4 days.

Nutrition Info:Per Serving: Total calories: 9; Total fat: 19g; Saturated fat: 4g; Sodium: 71mg; Carbohydrates: 55g; Fiber: 3g; Protein: 26g

Breakfast Bento Box

Servings: 2

Cooking Time: 12 Minutes

Ingredients:

- 2 eggs

- 2 ounces sliced prosciutto

- 20 small whole-grain crackers

- 20 whole, unsalted almonds (about ¼ cup)

- 2 (6-inch) Persian cucumbers, sliced

- 1 large pear, sliced

Directions:

1. Place the eggs in a saucepan and cover with water. Bring the water to a boil. As soon as the water starts to boil, place a lid on the pan and turn the heat off. Set a timer for minutes.

2. When the timer goes off, drain the hot water and run cold water over the eggs to cool. Peel the eggs when cool and cut in half.

3. Place 2 egg halves and half of the prosciutto, crackers, almonds, cucumber slices, and pear slices in each of 2 containers.

4. STORAGE: Store covered containers in the refrigerator for up to 5 days.

Nutrition Info:Per Serving: Total calories: 370; Total fat: 20g; Saturated fat: ; Sodium: 941mg; Carbohydrates: 35g; Fiber: 7g; Protein: 16g

Maple-cardamom Chia Pudding With Blueberries

Servings: 5

Cooking Time: 5 Minutes

Ingredients:

- 2½ cups low-fat (2%) milk

- ½ cup chia seeds

- 1 tablespoon plus 1 teaspoon pure maple syrup

- ¼ teaspoon ground cardamom

- 2½ cups frozen blueberries

Directions:

1. Place the milk, chia seeds, maple syrup, and cardamom in a large bowl and stir to combine.

2. Spoon ½ cup of the mixture into each of 5 containers.

3. Place ½ cup of frozen blueberries in each container and stir to combine. Let the pudding sit for at least an hour in the refrigerator before eating.

4. STORAGE: Store covered containers in the refrigerator for up to 5 days.

Nutrition Info:Per Serving: Total calories: 218; Total fat: 8g; Saturated fat: 2g; Sodium: 74mg; Carbohydrates: 28g; Fiber: 10g; Protein: 10g

Cheesy Bread

Servings: 12

Cooking Time: 15 Minutes

Ingredients:

- 3 cups shredded cheddar cheese

- 1 cup mayonnaise

- 1 1-ounce pack dry ranch dressing mix

- 1 2-ounce can chopped black olives, drained

- 4 green onions, sliced

- 2 French baguettes, cut into ½ inch slices

Directions:

1. Preheat oven to 350 degrees Fahrenheit.

2. In a medium-sized bowl, combine cheese, ranch dressing mix, mayonnaise, onions, and olives.

3. Increase mayo if you want a juicier mixture.

4. Spread cheese mixture on top of your French baguette slices.

5. Arrange the slices in a single layer on a large baking sheet.

6. Bake for about 15 minutes until the cheese is bubbly and browning.

7. Cool and chill.

8. Serve warm!

Nutrition Info:Per Serving: Calories: 2, Total Fat: 17 g, Saturated Fat: 7.2 g, Cholesterol: 35 mg, Sodium: 578 mg, Total Carbohydrate: 23.9 g, Dietary Fiber: 1.1 g, Total Sugars: 2.4 g, Protein: 11.1 g, Vitamin D: 3 mcg, Calcium: 229 mg, Iron: 2 mg, Potassium: 85 mg

Carrot-chickpea Fritters

Servings: 3

Cooking Time: 10 Minutes

Ingredients:

- 2 teaspoons olive oil, plus 1 tablespoon

- 3 cups shredded carrots

- 1 (4-ounce) bunch scallions, white and green parts chopped

- 1 (15-ounce) can low-sodium chickpeas, drained and rinsed

- ⅓ cup dried apricots (about 10 small apricot halves), chopped

- 1 teaspoon garlic powder

- 1½ teaspoons dried mint

- ⅓ cup chickpea flour

- 1 egg

- ¼ teaspoon kosher salt

- 1 tablespoon freshly squeezed lemon juice

- 1 (5-ounce) package arugula

- ¾ cup Garlic Yogurt Sauce

Directions:

1. Heat 2 teaspoons of oil in a -inch skillet over medium-high heat. Once the oil is hot, add the carrots and scallions, and cook for 5 minutes. Allow to cool.

2. While the carrots are cooking, mash the chickpeas in a large mixing bowl with the bottom of a coffee mug. (I find a coffee mug works better than a potato masher.)

3. Add the apricots, garlic powder, mint, chickpea flour, egg, salt, lemon juice, and cooked carrot

mixture to the bowl, and stir until well combined.

4. Form 6 patties and place them on a plate.

5. Heat the remaining 1 tablespoon of oil in the same skillet over medium-high heat. Once the oil is hot, add the patties. Cook for 3 minutes on each side, or until each side is browned.

6. Place 2 cooled fritters in each of 3 containers. Place about 2 cups of arugula in each of 3 other containers, and spoon ¼ cup Garlic Yogurt Sauce into each of 3 separate containers, or next to the arugula. The arugula and sauce are served at room temperature, while the fritters will be reheated.

7. STORAGE:Store covered containers in the refrigerator for up to 5 days. Uncooked patties can be frozen for 3 to 4 months.

Nutrition Info:Per Serving: Total calories: 461; Total fat: 17g; Saturated fat: 3g; Sodium: 393mg; Carbohydrates: 61g; Fiber: 15g; Protein: 21g

Whole-wheat Pasta With Lentil Bolognese

Servings: 4

Cooking Time: 55 Minutes

Ingredients:

- 2 tablespoons olive oil, divided

- 1 small yellow onion, chopped (about 2 cups)

- 1 tablespoon chopped garlic

- 2 medium carrots, peeled, halved vertically, and sliced (about 1¼ cup)

- 8 ounces button or cremini mushrooms, roughly chopped (about 4 cups)

- 1 teaspoon dried Italian herbs

- 2 tablespoons tomato paste

- ½ cup dry red wine

- 1 (28-ounce) can no-salt-added crushed tomatoes

- 2 cups water

- 1 cup uncooked brown lentils

- ½ teaspoon kosher salt

- 8 ounces dry whole-wheat penne pasta

- ¼ cup nutritional yeast

Directions:

1. Heat a soup pot on medium-high heat with tablespoon of oil. Once the oil is shimmering, add the onion and garlic, and cook for 2 minutes.

2. Add the carrots and mushrooms, then stir and cook for another 5 minutes.

3. Add the Italian herbs and tomato paste, stir to evenly incorporate, and cook for 5 more minutes, without stirring.

4. Add the wine and scrape up any bits from the bottom of the pan. Cook for 2 more minutes.

5. Add the tomatoes, water, lentils, and salt. Bring to a boil, then turn the heat down to low and simmer for 40 minutes.

6. While the sauce is cooking, cook the pasta according to the package directions, drain, and cool.

7. When the sauce is done simmering, stir in the remaining 1 tablespoon of oil and the nutritional yeast. Cool the sauce.

8. Combine 1 cup of cooked pasta and 1⅓ cups of sauce in each of 4 containers. Freeze the remaining sauce for a later meal.

9. STORAGE: Store covered containers in the refrigerator for up to 5 days.

Nutrition Info:Per Serving: Total calories: 570; Total fat: 9g; Saturated fat: 1g; Sodium: 435mg; Carbohydrates: 96g; Fiber: 17g; Protein: 27g

Strawberries With Cottage Cheese And Pistachios

Servings: 5

Cooking Time: 35 Minutes

Ingredients:

- 16 ounces low-fat cottage cheese

- 16 ounces strawberries, hulled and sliced

- ½ cup plus 2 tablespoons unsalted shelled pistachios

Directions:

1. Spoon ⅓ cup of cottage cheese into each of 5 containers.

2. Top each scoop of cottage cheese with ⅔ cup of strawberries and tablespoons of pistachios.

3. Refrigerate.

4. STORAGE: Store covered containers in the refrigerator for up to 5 days.

Nutrition Info:Per Serving: Total calories: 184; Total fat: 9g; Saturated fat: 2g; Sodium: 26g; Carbohydrates: 14g; Fiber: 4g; Protein: 15g

Turkey Meatballs With Tomato Sauce And Roasted Spaghetti Squash

Servings: 3

Cooking Time: 35 Minutes

Ingredients:

- FOR THE SPAGHETTI SQUASH

- 3 pounds spaghetti squash

- 1 teaspoon olive oil

- ¼ teaspoon kosher salt

- FOR THE MEATBALLS

- ½ pound lean ground turkey

- 4 ounces mushrooms, finely chopped (about 1½ cups)

- 2 tablespoons onion powder

- 1 tablespoon garlic powder

- 1 teaspoon dried Italian herbs

- ⅛ teaspoon kosher salt

- 1 large egg

- FOR THE SAUCE

- 1 (28-ounce) can crushed tomatoes

- 1 cup shredded carrots

- 1 teaspoon garlic powder

- 1 teaspoon onion powder

- ¼ teaspoon kosher salt

Directions:

1. TO MAKE THE SPAGHETTI SQUASH

2. Preheat the oven to 4°F and place a silicone baking mat or parchment paper on a sheet pan.

3. Using a heavy, sharp knife, cut the ends off the spaghetti squash. Stand the squash upright and cut down the middle. Scrape out the seeds and stringy flesh with a spoon and discard.

4. Rub the oil on the cut sides of the squash and sprinkle with the salt. Lay the squash cut-side down on the baking sheet. Roast for 30 to 35 minutes, until the flesh is tender when poked with a sharp knife.

5. When the squash is cool enough to handle, scrape the flesh out with a fork and place about 1 cup in each of 3 containers.

6. TO MAKE THE MEATBALLS AND SAUCE

7. Place all the ingredients for the meatballs in a large bowl. Mix with your hands until all the ingredients are combined.

8. Place all the sauce ingredients in an by-11-inch glass or ceramic baking dish, and stir to combine.

9. Form 12 golf-ball-size meatballs and place each directly in the baking dish of tomato sauce.

10. Place the baking dish in the oven and bake for 25 minutes. Cool.

11. Place 4 meatballs and 1 cup of sauce in each of the 3 squash containers.

12. STORAGE:Store covered containers in the refrigerator for up to 5 days.

Nutrition Info:Per Serving: Total calories: 406; Total fat: ; Saturated fat: 5g; Sodium: 1,296mg; Carbohydrates: 45g; Fiber: 10g; Protein: 29g

Salmon Cakes With Steamed Green Bean Gremolata

Servings: 4

Cooking Time: 6 Minutes

Ingredients:

- 2 (6-ounce) cans skinless, boneless salmon, drained

- ½ teaspoon garlic powder

- ⅓ cup minced shallot

- 2 tablespoons Dijon mustard

- 2 eggs

- ½ cup panko bread crumbs

- 1 tablespoon capers, chopped

- 1 cup chopped parsley

- ⅓ cup chopped sun-dried tomatoes

- 1 tablespoon freshly squeezed lemon juice

- 1 tablespoon olive oil

- Zest of 2 lemons (about 2 tablespoons when zested with a Microplane)

- ¼ cup minced parsley

- 1 teaspoon minced garlic

- ¼ teaspoon kosher salt

- 1 teaspoon olive oil

- 1 pound green beans, trimmed

Directions:

1. TO MAKE THE SALMON CAKES

2. In a large bowl, place the salmon, garlic, shallot, mustard, eggs, bread crumbs, capers, parsley, tomatoes, and lemon juice. Stir well to combine.

3. Form 8 patties and place them on a plate.

4. Heat the oil in a 12-inch skillet over medium-high heat. Once the oil is hot, add the patties. Cook for 3 minutes on each side, or until each side is browned.

5. Place 2 cooled salmon cakes in each of 4 containers.

6. TO MAKE THE GREEN BEANS

7. In a small bowl, combine the lemon zest, parsley, garlic, salt, and oil.

8. Bring about ¼ to ½ inch of water to a boil in a soup pot, Dutch oven, or skillet.

9. Once the water is boiling, add the green beans, cover, and set a timer for 3 minutes. The green beans should be crisp-tender.

10. Drain the green beans and transfer to a large bowl. Add the gremolata (lemon zest mixture) and toss to combine.

11. Divide the green beans among the 4 salmon cake containers. If using, place ¼ cup of Garlic Yogurt Sauce in each of 4 sauce containers. Refrigerate.

12. STORAGE: Store covered containers in the refrigerator for up to 5 days. Uncooked patties can be frozen for 3 to 4 months.

Nutrition Info:Per Serving: Total calories: 268; Total fat: 9g; Saturated fat: 2g; Sodium: 638mg; Carbohydrates: 21g; Fiber: 6g; Protein: 27g

Popcorn Trail Mix

Servings: 5

Cooking Time: 35 Minutes

Ingredients:

- 12 dried apricot halves, quartered

- ⅔ cup whole, unsalted almonds

- ½ cup green pumpkin seeds (pepitas)

- 4 cups air-popped lightly salted popcorn

Directions:

1. Place the apricots, almonds, and pumpkin seeds in a medium bowl and toss with clean hands to evenly mix.

2. Scoop about ⅓ cup of the mixture into each of 5 containers or resealable sandwich bags. Place ¾ cup of popcorn in each of 5 separate

containers or resealable bags. You will have one extra serving.

3. Mix the popcorn and the almond mixture together when it's time to eat. (The apricots make the popcorn stale quickly, which is why they're stored separately.)

4. STORAGE: Store covered containers or resealable bags at room temperature for up to 5 days.

Nutrition Info:Per Serving: Total calories: 244; Total fat: 16g; Saturated fat: 2g; Sodium: 48mg; Carbohydrates: 19g; Fiber: ; Protein: 10g

Creamy Shrimp-stuffed Portobello Mushrooms

Servings: 3

Cooking Time: 40 Minutes

Ingredients:

- 1 teaspoon olive oil, plus 2 tablespoons

- 6 portobello mushrooms, caps and stems separated and stems chopped

- 6 ounces broccoli florets, finely chopped (about 2 cups)

- 2 teaspoons chopped garlic

- 10 ounces uncooked peeled, deveined shrimp, thawed if frozen, roughly chopped

- 1 (14.5-ounce) can no-salt-added diced tomatoes

- 4 tablespoons roughly chopped fresh basil

- ½ cup mascarpone cheese

- ¼ cup panko bread crumbs

- 4 tablespoons grated Parmesan, divided

- ¼ teaspoon kosher salt

Directions:

1. Preheat the oven to 350°F. Line a sheet pan with a silicone baking mat or parchment paper.

2. Rub 1 teaspoon of oil over the bottom (stem side) of the mushroom caps and place on the lined sheet pan, stem-side up.

3. Heat the remaining 2 tablespoons of oil in a 12-inch skillet on medium-high heat. Once the oil is shimmering, add the chopped mushroom stems and broccoli, and sauté for 2 to minutes. Add the garlic and shrimp, and continue cooking for 2 more minutes.

4. Add the tomatoes, basil, mascarpone, bread crumbs, 3 tablespoons of Parmesan, and the salt. Stir to combine and turn the heat off.

5. With the mushroom cap openings facing up, mound slightly less than 1 cup of filling into each mushroom. Top each with ½ teaspoon of the remaining Parmesan cheese.

6. Bake the mushrooms for 35 minutes.

7. Place 2 mushroom caps in each of 3 containers.

8. STORAGE: Store covered containers in the refrigerator for up to 4 days.

Nutrition Info:Per Serving: Total calories: 47 Total fat: 31g; Saturated fat: 10g; Sodium: 526mg; Carbohydrates: 26g; Fiber: 7g; Protein: 26g

Rosemary Edamame, Zucchini, And Sun-dried Tomatoes With Garlic-chive Quinoa

Servings: 4

Cooking Time: 15 Minutes

Ingredients:

- FOR THE GARLIC-CHIVE QUINOA

- 1 teaspoon olive oil

- 1 teaspoon chopped garlic

- ⅔ cup quinoa

- 1⅓ cups water

- ¼ teaspoon kosher salt

- 1 (¾-ounce) package fresh chives, chopped

- FOR THE ROSEMARY EDAMAME, ZUCCHINI, AND SUN-DRIED TOMATOES

- 1 teaspoon oil from sun-dried tomato jar

- 2 medium zucchini, cut in half lengthwise and sliced into half-moons (about 3 cups)

- 1 (12-ounce) package frozen shelled edamame, thawed (2 cups)

- ½ cup julienne-sliced sun-dried tomatoes in olive oil, drained

- ¼ teaspoon dried rosemary

- ⅛ teaspoon kosher salt

Directions:

1. TO MAKE THE GARLIC-CHIVE QUINOA

2. Heat the oil over medium heat in a saucepan. Once the oil is shimmering, add the garlic and cook for 1 minute, stirring often so it doesn't burn.

3. Add the quinoa and stir a few times. Add the water and salt and turn the heat up to high.

Once the water is boiling, cover the pan and turn the heat down to low. Simmer the quinoa for 15 minutes, or until the water is absorbed.

4. Stir in the chives and fluff the quinoa with a fork.

5. Place ½ cup quinoa in each of 4 containers.

6. TO MAKE THE ROSEMARY EDAMAME, ZUCCHINI, AND SUN-DRIED TOMATOES

7. Heat the oil in a 12-inch skillet over medium-high heat. Once the oil is shimmering, add the zucchini and cook for 2 minutes.

8. Add the edamame, sun-dried tomatoes, rosemary, and salt, and cook for another 6 minutes, or until the zucchini is crisp-tender.

9. Spoon 1 cup of the edamame mixture into each of the 4 quinoa containers.

10. STORAGE: Store covered containers in the refrigerator for up to 5 days.

110

Nutrition Info:Per Serving: Total calories: 312; Total fat: ; Saturated fat: 1g; Sodium: 389mg; Carbohydrates: 39g; Fiber: 9g; Protein: 15g

Cherry, Vanilla, And Almond Overnight Oats

Servings: 5

Cooking Time: 10 Minutes

Ingredients:

- 1⅔ cups rolled oats

- 3⅓ cups unsweetened vanilla almond milk

- 5 tablespoons plain, unsalted almond butter

- 2 teaspoons vanilla extract

- 1 tablespoon plus 2 teaspoons pure maple syrup

- 3 tablespoons chia seeds

- ½ cup plus 2 tablespoons sliced almonds

- 1⅔ cups frozen sweet cherries

Directions:

1. In a large bowl, mix the oats, almond milk, almond butter, vanilla, maple syrup, and chia seeds until well combined.

2. Spoon ¾ cup of the oat mixture into each of 5 containers.

3. Top each serving with 2 tablespoons of almonds and ⅓ cup of cherries.

4. STORAGE: Store covered containers in the refrigerator for up to 5 days. Overnight oats can be eaten cold or warmed up in the microwave.

Nutrition Info:Per Serving: Total calories: 373; Total fat: 20g; Saturated fat: 1g; Sodium: 121mg; Carbohydrates: 40g; Fiber: 11g; Protein: 13g

Rotisserie Chicken, Baby Kale, Fennel, And Green Apple Salad

Servings: 3

Cooking Time: 15 Minutes

Ingredients:

- 1 teaspoon olive oil

- 1 teaspoon chopped garlic

- ⅔ cup quinoa

- 1⅓ cups water

- 1 cooked rotisserie chicken, meat removed and shredded (about 9 ounces)

- 1 fennel bulb, core and fronds removed, thinly sliced (about 2 cups)

- 1 small green apple, julienned (about 1½ cups)

- 8 tablespoons Honey-Lemon Vinaigrette, divided

- 1 (5-ounce) package baby kale

- 6 tablespoons walnut pieces

Directions:

1. Heat the oil over medium heat in a saucepan. Once the oil is shimmering, add the garlic and cook for minute, stirring often so that it doesn't burn.

2. Add the quinoa and stir a few times. Add the water and turn the heat up to high. Once the water is boiling, cover the pan and turn the heat down to low. Simmer the quinoa for 15 minutes, or until the water is absorbed. Cool.

3. Place the chicken, fennel, apple, and cooled quinoa in a large bowl. Add 2 tablespoons of the vinaigrette to the bowl and mix to combine.

4. Divide the baby kale, chicken mixture, and walnuts among 3 containers. Pour 2 tablespoons of the remaining vinaigrette into each of 3 sauce containers.

5. STORAGE: Store covered containers in the refrigerator for up to days.

Nutrition Info:Per Serving: Total calories: 9; Total fat: 39g; Saturated fat: 6g; Sodium: 727mg; Carbohydrates: 49g; Fiber: 8g; Protein: 29g

Roasted Za'atar Salmon With Peppers And Sweet Potatoes

Servings: 4

Cooking Time: 25 Minutes

Ingredients:

- FOR THE VEGGIES

- 2 large red bell peppers, cut into ½-inch strips

- 1 pound sweet potatoes, peeled and cut into 1-inch chunks

- 1 tablespoon olive oil

- ¼ teaspoon kosher salt

- FOR THE SALMON

- 2¾ teaspoons sesame seeds

- 2¾ teaspoons dried thyme leaves

- 2¾ teaspoons sumac

- 1 pound skinless, boneless salmon fillet, divided into 4 pieces

- ⅛ teaspoon kosher salt

- 1 teaspoon olive oil

- 2 teaspoons freshly squeezed lemon juice

Directions:

1. TO MAKE THE VEGGIES

2. Preheat the oven to 4°F.

3. Place silicone baking mats or parchment paper on two sheet pans.

4. On the first pan, place the peppers and sweet potatoes. Pour the oil and sprinkle the salt over both and toss to coat. Spread everything out in an even layer. Place the sheet pan in the oven and set a timer for 10 minutes.

5. TO MAKE THE SALMON

6. Mix the sesame seeds, thyme, and sumac together in a small bowl to make the za'atar spice mix.

7. Place the salmon fillets on the second sheet pan. Sprinkle the salt evenly across the fillets. Spread ¼ teaspoon of oil and ½ teaspoon of lemon juice over each piece of salmon.

8. Pat 2 teaspoons of the za'atar spice mix over each piece of salmon.

9. When the veggie timer goes off, place the salmon in the oven with the veggies and bake for 10 minutes for salmon that is ½ inch thick and for 15 minutes for salmon that is 1 inch thick. The veggies should be done when the salmon is done cooking.

10. Place one quarter of the veggies and 1 piece of salmon in each of 4 separate containers.

11. STORAGE:Store covered containers in the refrigerator for up to 4 days.

Nutrition Info:Per Serving: Total calories: 295; Total fat: 10g; Saturated fat: 2g; Sodium: 249mg; Carbohydrates: 29g; Fiber: 6g; Protein: 25g

28-Day Meal Plan

Day 1

Breakfast: Cauliflower Fritters With Hummus

Lunch: Marinated Tuna Steak

Dinner: Garlic And Shrimp Pasta

Day 2

Breakfast: Italian Breakfast Sausage With Baby Potatoes And Vegetables

Lunch: Paprika Butter Shrimps

Dinner: Mediterranean Avocado Salmon Salad

Day 3

Breakfast: Greek Quinoa Breakfast Bowl

Lunch: Moroccan Fish

Dinner: Beet Kale Salad

Day 4

Breakfast: Egg, Prosciutto, And Cheese Freezer Sandwiches

Lunch: Grilled Lamb Chops

Dinner: Niçoise-inspired Salad With Sardines

Day 5

Breakfast: Healthy Zucchini Kale Tomato Salad

Lunch: Broiled Chili Calamari

Dinner: Mediterranean Chicken Pasta Bake

Day 6

Breakfast: Cheese And Cauliflower Frittata With Peppers

Lunch: Seafood Paella

Dinner: Mediterranean Pearl Couscous

Day 7

Breakfast: Avocado Kale Omelet

Lunch: Greek-style Braised Pork With Leeks, Greens, And Potatoes

Dinner: Delicious Broccoli Tortellini Salad

Day 8

Breakfast: Mediterranean Breakfast Burrito

Lunch: Greek Baked Cod

Dinner: Quinoa Stuffed Eggplant With Tahini Sauce

Day 9

Breakfast: Spinach, Feta And Egg Breakfast Quesadillas

Lunch: Zoodles With Turkey Meatballs

Dinner: Lettuce Tomato Salad

Day 10

Breakfast: Egg-topped Quinoa Bowl With Kale

Lunch: Lasagna

Dinner: Cheese Onion Soup

Day 11

Breakfast: Strawberry Greek Frozen Yogurt

Lunch: Tuna With Vegetable Mix

Dinner: Mixed Spice Burgers

Day 12

Breakfast: Almond Peach Oatmeal

Lunch: Pistachio Sole Fish

Dinner: Beef Tomato Soup

Day 13

Breakfast: Peanut Butter Banana Pudding

Lunch: Baked Tilapia

Dinner: A Great Mediterranean Snapper

Day 14

Breakfast: Raspberry-lemon Olive Oil Muffins

Lunch: Italian Skillet Chicken With Mushrooms And Tomatoes

Dinner: Mediterranean Pizza

Day 15

Breakfast: Pearl Couscous Salad

Lunch: Herbal Lamb Cutlets With Roasted Veggies

Dinner: Roasted Vegetable Quinoa Bowl

Day 16

Breakfast: Mushroom Tomato Egg Cups

Lunch: Heartthrob Mediterranean Tilapia

Dinner: Tabouli Salad

Day 17

Breakfast: Mediterranean Breakfast Salad

Lunch: Beef Sausage Pancakes

Dinner: Greek Lemon Chicken Soup

Day 18

Breakfast: Breakfast Carrot Oatmeal

Lunch: Mediterranean-style Pesto Chicken

Dinner: Lobster Salad

Day 19

Breakfast: Rum-raisin Arborio Pudding

Lunch: Italian Tuna Sandwiches

Dinner: Chicken Lentil Soup

Day 20

Breakfast: Mediterranean Quinoa And Feta Egg Muffins

Lunch: Mediterranean Baked Sole Fillet

Dinner: Luncheon Fancy Salad

Day 21

Breakfast: Vegetable Breakfast Bowl

Lunch: North African–inspired Sautéed Shrimp With Leeks And Peppers

Dinner: Salmon Skillet Dinner

Day 22

Breakfast: Egg-artichoke Breakfast Casserole

Lunch: Red Wine–braised Pot Roast With Carrots And Mushrooms

Dinner: Italian Platter

Day 23

Breakfast: Breakfast Cauliflower Rice Bowl

Lunch: Garlic And Cajun Shrimp Bowl With Noodles

Dinner: Grilled Salmon Tzatziki Bowl

Day 24

Breakfast: Savory Cucumber-dill Yogurt

Lunch: Smoky Chickpea, Chard, And Butternut Squash Soup

Dinner: Mediterranean Potato Salad

Day 25

Breakfast: Zucchini Pudding

Lunch: Crispy Baked Chicken

Dinner: Italian Baked Beans

Day 26

Breakfast: Healthy Dry Fruit Porridge

Lunch: Moroccan Spiced Stir-fried Beef With Butternut Squash And Chickpeas

Dinner: Greek Chicken Wraps

Day 27

Breakfast: Peach Blueberry Oatmeal

Lunch: Italian Chicken With Sweet Potato And Broccoli

Dinner: Vegetable Soup

Day 28

Breakfast: Tahini Egg Salad With Pita

Lunch: Herb-crusted Halibut

Dinner: Spinach And Beans Mediterranean Style Salad

Conclusion

Have you managed to conquer the woman or man of your dreams?

Have I succeeded with this cookbook to make you prepare wonderful dinners?

I have presented you with the best recipes, the tastiest and easiest to prepare, and now they are at your disposal.

Make good use of them, train every day and you will see the results.

Thank you for following me.